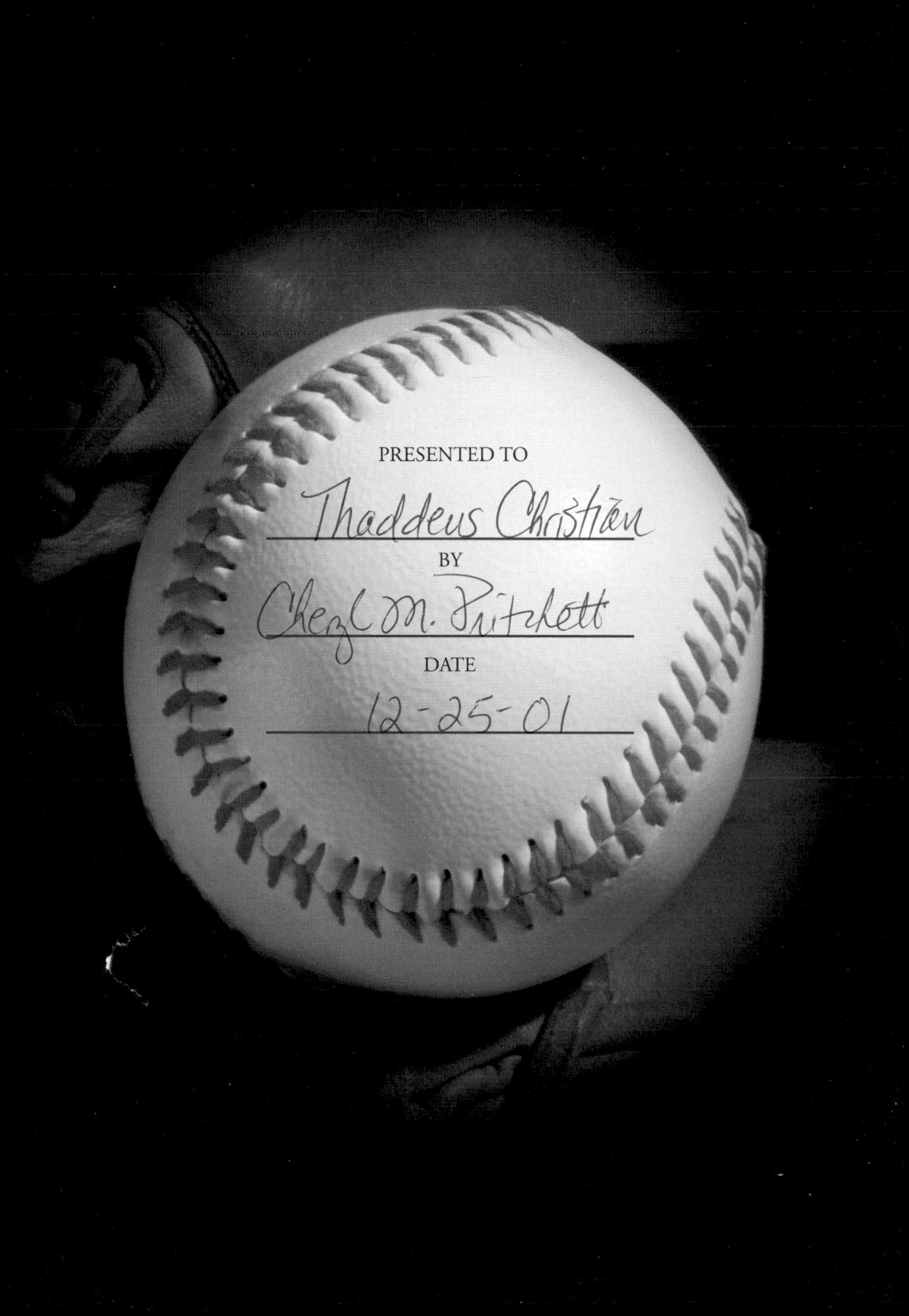

PRESENTED TO

Thaddeus Christian

BY

Cheryl M. Pritchett

DATE

12-25-01

PLAY BALL

BY **Dave Dravecky**

with Mike Yorkey

J. Countryman
Nashville, Tennessee

Unless otherwise noted, all Scripture quotations in this book are from the New King James
Version of the Bible (NKJV), copyright © 1979, 1980, 1982, Thomas Nelson, Inc., Publishers.

J. Countryman® is a trademark of Thomas Nelson Inc.

Designed by Koechel Peterson and Associates, Minneapolis, Minnesota

Project editor: Jenny Baumgartner
Special thanks to Rev. Hugh E. Baumgartner Jr.

Photo Credits:
Copyright © Joel Zwink/Zwink Photography – Cover, Back Cover, Endpapers, 2-3, 4-5, 6-7, 8, 10, 12, 14,
16-17, 22, 25, 26-27, 32, 35, 36-37, 45, 46-47, 51, 56-57, 61, 66-67, 68, 71, 76-77,
82, 85, 86-87, 96-97, 102, 108, 116, 120, 123, 124-125.
Copyright © 2001 Dave Dravecky's Outreach of Hope ministry 119.

28 © Vince Streano/CORBIS; 72, 88 © Reuters New Media Inc./CORBIS;
110-111 © Royalty Free/CORBIS; 112 © Philip James Corwin/CORBIS;
18, 38, 42, 48, 52, 58, 62, 78, 92, 98, 104 © Bettmann/CORBIS;
129 © Ed Eckstein/CORBIS.

ISBN: 0-8499-5752-4

Published in association with the literary agency of Alive Communications,
1465 Kelly Johnson Blvd., Suite 320, Colorado Springs, Colorado 80920

Printed and bound in Belgium

www.jcountryman.com

Table of Contents

Dedication

To my father, Frank Dravecky, who taught me so much on the field and off the field. Dad, thanks for helping me to remember that baseball is a kid's game and for teaching me that whatever I do in life, I should have fun and do it to the best of my ability.

Acknowledgements

I would also like to thank Mike Yorkey for his incredible assistance with the research and writing of this book and Rick Myatt, a San Diego pastor, for his assistance with the choosing of the scriptural quotations.

FOREWORD
by Randy Johnson

*I*f you walked into the basement of my Phoenix home, I think you would be surprised. You won't discover any of my Cy Young awards, but you will find my collection of autographs, which includes Cy Young, Lefty Grove, Babe Ruth, and every Cy Young award winner from each league over the past ten years.

I love the history of the game, and I enjoy learning what these old-timers have done. One of my prized autographs comes from Kid Nichols. Did you know that he was the only pitcher to win thirty games seven times? I didn't either, which means that having a memento of Kids Nichols gives me an appreciation for what the great players accomplished before my time.

These days, I'm greatly humbled by what I've been able to accomplish between the lines. I've been a big-league pitcher for thirteen years and a Christian for seven years. With each passing season, I'm realizing that any history I'm making has not been done by my own strength. The Lord has taught me to accept the peaks and valleys and try to do my best—to get the most out of my ability. I understand that the Lord is in charge of our destiny and that the blessings I've been given could come and go at any moment. That knowledge has helped me mentally prepare to be the best pitcher I can be.

I promise you that you're going to like this book by Dave Dravecky, one of the most courageous men I know. I hope that Dave doesn't take this wrong, but he has delivered a fat pitch of a book. You'll put some solid wood on his offering as you enjoy reading this beautifully produced book.

Play Ball tells great stories from baseball's storied past and offers spiritual points that we can all take to heart. You're going to touch all the bases by the time you're finished.

RANDY JOHNSON

Dave Dravecki

Introduction
THE FIRST PITCH

Many of us grew up playing baseball, whether it was impromptu whiffle ball games in the backyard or organized Little League games on chalk-lined fields where our parents yelled encouragement from the grandstands.

When the umpire yelled, "Play ball!" we knew exactly what that meant. We knew where to take our positions, how to hold and waggle our bats, and how to run the bases. All of it was ingrained into us. We may not have known all the rules—why else would three runners end up at third base?—but we learned how to play baseball the right way. If we stuck with the game as a player or a fan during our teen years, we began to understand the intricacies of America's oldest and most complex sport.

Baseball operates under the *Official Baseball Rules,* a dry-as-toast legalistic document full of do's and don'ts. Known as "The Book," it begins by stating that baseball is a game "between two teams of nine players each, under the direction of a manager, played on an enclosed field in accordance of these rules, under the jurisdiction of one or more umpires."

Ah, but baseball is much more than that. Baseball is Mark McGwire and Sammy Sosa giving us a home run duel for the ages in 1998. Baseball is Bill Buckner letting a slow grounder roll under his glove, costing the Boston Red Sox the 1986 World Series against the New York Mets. Baseball is:

- Carlton Fisk waving for his home run ball to stay fair.
- Tom Seaver and the "Miracle Mets" of 1969.
- Mantle and Maris in 1961.

- Joe DiMaggio passing the torch.

- Ted Williams going 6-for-8 on the final day of the 1941 season to bat .406.

- Babe Ruth's "called shot" in the 1932 World Series against the Chicago Cubs.

- History's greatest team—the 1927 New York Yankees.

- Tinker to Evers to Chance.

I grew up with this baseball lore, thanks to my father. Dad had a great love for the game, and he believed what happened between the lines applied to life as well. "There are two things to remember," I can still hear Dad saying. "Whatever you choose to do, work hard at it. Don't shortchange yourself; be the best you can be. But more important, go out and have fun."

The latter advice was put to the test during my junior year at Youngstown State University. I was consumed by baseball, and I wanted to become a major league pitcher in the worst way. My win-loss record that year was 7-1 with a very stingy 0.88 earned-run average. My strong pitching helped Youngstown State to the NCAA Division II baseball tournament for the first time in school history.

Our first playoff game was against Wright State University, and I was handed the game ball. "Go get 'em," said my manager, Dom Roselli, and I confidently took the mound, ready to show Wright State some of my heat and the two-dozen major league scouts in the stands that I was the next Sandy Koufax or Vida Blue.

Each pitch I threw seemed to find the batter's sweet spot on the bat. Singles, doubles, and home runs rained all over the field. As each run crossed the plate, the opposing players heaped scorn in my direction. "Hey, Dravecky, your ERA is now 1.4 and rising!" My manager finally sent me to the showers in the third inning after I gave up nine runs, eight earned. I hung my head during the long walk to the dugout. No baseball scouts would be talking to me after the game, which we finally lost 26-1.

Success had become more important to me than having fun. I was so focused on impressing the scouts that I put too much stress on myself. I pitched poorly.

I approached my senior year of baseball with a different attitude. I wanted to get back to playing a kid's game. Since I wasn't going anywhere, I would play baseball for the game's sake. I had a blast all season long. Just before my college career ended, I pitched against Clarion State, hurling a three-hit, seven-inning shutout while striking out fourteen players. Two scouts were in the stands—one representing the Los Angeles Dodgers, the other from the Pittsburgh Pirates organization. When the Pirates drafted me (a surprise, I might add), little did I know that God had an amazing future in front of me.

Maybe that's why I like baseball so much. This special game has many parallels with our Christian life. We all get our at-bats; it's what we do with them that counts. We need signs from the third-base coach, just as we need signs and advice from God's Word. We need to concentrate on hitting and take our hacks, just as we need to concentrate on Jesus as we go to bat for Him. We need to run everything out and take the extra base when we can, just as we must take the opportunity to share Christ with others when given the chance. We need to run for home and be prepared to slide, just as we need to keep our eyes on Jesus and be prepared for our heavenly reward.

That's why you're going to enjoy this book. Many of life's lessons have already taken place on the ball field, and we can apply them to our spiritual lives as well. Just as the Chicago Cubs' Ernie Banks is famous for saying, "It's a great day. Let's play two," you're going to want to reread *Play Ball* again and again.

DAVE DRAVECKY

1st Inning

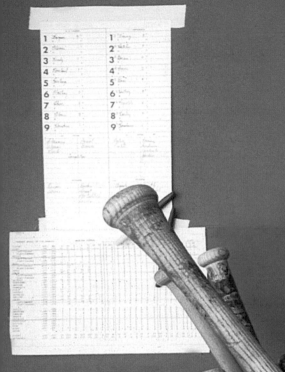

Top of the First
OPENING DAY

hat is it about Opening Day that stirs the souls of baseball fans? Is it the pageantry, Marine color guard, and rousing player introductions? Is it the peanuts, popcorn, and Cracker Jack? Dodger dogs and Brewer brats?

The Opening Day tradition was born in 1910 when umpire Billy Evans asked William Howard Taft, the president of the United States, if he would honor those in attendance by throwing the "first ball." Taft lobbed one to Washington pitcher Walter "Big Train" Johnson, who proceeded to toss a one-hit shutout against the Philadelphia Athletics.

Down through the years, every U.S. president except Jimmy Carter has thrown out the first pitch. Bill Clinton, not content to lazily toss a ball from the stands, promised that he would "burn it in there" when he took the mound at Camden Yards in Baltimore.

No other sport has an Opening Day tradition like baseball. The opening kickoff of the NFL season doesn't offer the same anticipation as the first pitch in baseball, and the man on the street couldn't tell you if the NBA season starts in October or November. (The answer is November.)

Baseball's Opening Day signals the start of a new season, a time when everyone starts with a clean slate, and every team can talk about their hopes and dreams.

I'll never forget the only time I was tabbed to be the Opening Day pitcher. The season was 1988, and the San Francisco Giants handed me the ball against the Los Angeles Dodgers in a packed Chavez Ravine. Starting for the Dodgers was Fernando Valenzuela, the premier left-handed pitcher in the National League. "Fernandomania" still reigned in those days.

We didn't touch him in the first inning. Then it was my turn to take the mound in the bottom of the first. The butterflies in my stomach were fluttering fast and furiously, but I was ready for the Dodgers first batter, second baseman Steve Sax.

I leaned in and looked for a sign. My catcher, Bob Melvin, put down a single finger, then pointed toward the batter, signaling for an inside fastball. That was fine with me. Throughout my career, my bread-and-butter pitch was a cut fastball on the inside part of the plate. That pitch on the fists had broken the bats of many right-handed hitters. My left foot swept the rubber as I gathered my thoughts. I looked at Sax digging in for my first pitch of the season and thought to myself, *Okay, Buddy, here comes my cut fastball on the inside of the dish.*

There are Opening Day pitchers and pitchers who start on Opening Day.

ROGER CRAIG,
MY SAN FRANCISCO GIANTS MANAGER

Sax swung from the heels and hammered a line-drive home run into the left field bleachers, sending the Dodger fans into a frenzy. What a way to start the season! While Sax rounded the bases, I gathered my thoughts.

It's only one hit, only one run, I said to myself, as I threw my rosin bag to the ground. *Let's settle down. We have nine more innings to play.*

From that point on, I tossed a three-hit, complete game shutout—even doubling off Fernando—on the way to a 5-1 victory. What I learned that afternoon was that one pitch in the first inning doesn't make a game. There was still a lot of baseball to play.

What about you? Are you going through life haunted by something that happened to you years ago? Do you feel like there's no hope? Perhaps you wonder if your past mistakes disqualify you from serving on God's team.

Wonder no longer. Because of God's great love and mercy, it is never too late to get in the game. No matter what has happened in your past, God can wipe the slate clean and give you a new Opening Day—a future that is bright and enthusiasm that is high. Start off the season of your life today by seeking God's plan for you. You'll be glad you hung in there, just as I did in Los Angeles.

Brethren, I do not count myself to have apprehended; but one thing I do, forgetting those things which are behind and reaching forward to those things which are ahead, I press toward the goal for the prize of the upward call of God in Christ Jesus.

PHILIPPIANS 3:13–14

Bottom of the First
"AND LEADING OFF..."

ajor league ball clubs usually score more runs in the first inning than any other inning. As Yankee manager Casey Stengel used to say, "You can look it up."

Reason? I can tell you from a pitcher's standpoint that my nervous energy intensifies when the first batter is announced and I hear the decibel count rise. The leadoff hitter—usually a small, wiry second baseman or a rangy shortstop—spends the first fifteen seconds messing up the lines in the batter's box and digging a hole with his rear foot. He's eager to get going, but he's also eager to make you pitch to him. Most lead-off hitters come to the plate with a disciplined strike zone.

From the hitter's standpoint, the first inning is the "structured" inning. The manager starts with the top of the order, pitting a patient, solid-contact leadoff man with speed and bat control against a pitcher attempting to find his stride. The leadoff batter is followed by a number-two man, who can hit-and-run or work the count. This allows the leadoff man to get a big jump stealing second base. Many number-two hitters have a knack for fouling off pitches, which aggravates pitchers.

The number-three hitter is almost always reserved for the biggest bopper on the team who is not necessarily the best hitter for average. Mark McGwire, Sammy Sosa, and Ken Griffey Jr. are your classic number-three hitters. Their ability to "go yard" or hit towering home runs has pitchers shivering in their cleats. Waiting in the on-deck circle is the number-four hitter—the clean-up man—who conceivably could be asked to clear the bases if he comes up with the bases loaded.

Teams blessed with power hitters have the upper hand, which is why the 1927 New York Yankees 3-4-5 lineup of Babe Ruth,

Lou Gehrig, and Bob Meusel was known as the heart of "Murderer's Row." Pitchers were understandably reluctant to pitch around Babe Ruth when they knew Lou Gehrig was swinging two bats in the on-deck circle.

I wonder what it would have been like to pitch against the Babe, a left-handed hitter. I was a lefty, so I would have had some statistical advantage against baseball's greatest player. Going against the best with the ball in my hand, a bat in his, would have been a superb match-up. That's what makes baseball a great game.

> *Hitting the ball was easy. Running around the bases was the tough part.*
>
> MICKEY MANTLE

No matter where you are with God, this is a fantastic time to lead off with Him. He's "structured" a great life for you, giving you a wonderful opportunity to step up to the plate and take your hacks. He has put you in the perfect place in His lineup.

All too often we compare ourselves with others and see nothing but shortcomings. We wish we were wittier, more intelligent, better looking—or we dream of being all-star baseball players. But God has a place for you—a place perfectly suited for your abilities and personality.

When I lost my arm to cancer, I wondered if God still had a role for me, a place in His batting order. I needn't have worried. God had a spot reserved for me, which is ministering to cancer patients.

I know He has a place that is special and unique to you, a spot that has significance for eternity. It is only when we reflect upon this truth that we can truly be at peace with ourselves, secure in God's strategy.

His plan for your life begins today, so go grab a bat.

"Batter up!"

Mark McGwire

I will praise You, for I am fearfully and wonderfully made; marvelous are Your works, and that my soul knows very well. My frame was not hidden from You, when I was made in secret, and skillfully wrought in the lowest parts of the earth. Your eyes saw my substance, being yet unformed. And in Your book they all were written, the days fashioned for me, when as yet there were none of them.

PSALM 139:14–16

2nd Inning

Top of the Second
THE SERMON
ON THE MOUND

I've seen it happen a hundred times: a young pitcher works his way to the major leagues, and then forgets what brought him there.

He starts out like he's pitching on a mound of eggshells. He walks the first batter of the inning, fails to keep runners close, and forgets to cover first base on bunts. Instead of challenging hitters *mano a mano,* he nibbles at the corners, falls behind in the count, and lays a fat one over the plate on a 3-1 pitch. He drives his manager crazy and gives his pitching coach a bad case of indigestion.

Orel Hershiser, a wonderful Christian brother and a future Hall of Fame shoo-in, was one of those pitchers when he was called up by the Los Angeles Dodgers in 1984. During his first full season, Orel was relegated to the bullpen, where he worked middle relief. He didn't see much action, but when his number was called, he pitched carefully—and inconsistently. His specialty became the bases-empty two-out walk, followed by the man-on-first-base two-out walk, followed by the two-run double, followed by handing the ball to the manager and taking an early shower.

Even back then, Orel was outspoken about his faith, so it was whispered that he was just another "wimpy" Christian athlete, a passive, let-it-happen kind of guy who didn't have the guts to challenge hitters. In the midst of his struggles, saddled by a 6.20 ERA, Orel got bad news prior to a game: manager Tommy Lasorda wanted to see him in his office. Orel figured that he would be handed a one-way ticket to Albuquerque, home of the Dodgers AAA club.

Tommy Lasorda was the loud, brash skipper who claimed that he bled Dodger blue. No, he wasn't going to send Orel down; he was going to light a fire under him. (You're about to read the PG version.)

Tommy began slowly, recalling Orel's last disastrous outing against the Houston Astros. Two men on, two out. Jose Cruz, a left-handed talented contact hitter, at the plate.

"You throw low and away, ball one," began Lasorda. "Then low and away, ball two. Low and away, ball three. You know he's takin', but you still throw low and away, but lucky for you, it's called a strike. He knows you can't afford to walk him, so he's sittin' on your 3-1 pitch, and what do you do?"

Orel stood there, shifting his weight from foot to foot. This was painful. Tommy's face reddened as he burst out in fury, "You laid the ball in for him! Boom! Double and two runs! Hershiser, you're giving these hitters too much credit! You're tellin' yourself, 'If I throw this ball over the plate, they're gonna hit it out.'"

> *A life is not important except in the impact it has on other lives.*
>
> JACKIE ROBINSON

Tommy was just getting warmed up. "You don't believe in yourself! You're scared to pitch in the big leagues! Who do you think these hitters are, Babe Ruth? Ruth's dead! You've got good stuff. If you didn't, I wouldn't have brought you up. Quit bein' so careful! Go after the hitter! Get ahead in the count! Take charge! Be aggressive! Be a bulldog out there! That's gonna be your new name: Bulldog. From now on, you're going to be known as Bulldog Hershiser!"

The rest, as we know, is great history. Tommy's impassioned speech revolutionized Orel's attitude. He went after hitters, got ahead in the counts, and acted like he belonged in The Show. He acted like a big league pitcher because he *believed* that he was a big league pitcher.

How do you act as a Christian? Are you a wimpy Christian who's afraid to articulate what you believe in a culture that is not friendly to biblical values? Are you afraid to make your best pitch and let the chips fall where they may? Or do you nibble at the corners, hoping that your stuff is acceptable to the world?

Orel's problem was fear. He was afraid to challenge the hitters, afraid his stuff just wasn't good enough. When he put away his fear and replaced it with confidence in his ability, he became one of the best pitchers of the last twenty years. His record of fifty-nine consecutive shutout innings, set in 1988, will probably never be broken.

Too often, we throw away our confidence in Christ and let fear have its way when it should be the other away around. We *can* get ahead of fear in the count, then strike it out.

For God has not given us a spirit of fear, but of power and of love and of a sound mind. Therefore do not be ashamed of the testimony of our Lord, nor of me His prisoner, but share with me in the sufferings for the gospel according to the power of God.

2 TIMOTHY 1:7–8

Bottom of the Second
BECOMING A "FIVE TOOL" PLAYER

hey are called "complete packages" or "franchise players"—those who can run, catch, throw, hit for power, and hit for average. Only a select few ballplayers can claim the "five tool" mantle. Many baseball historians favor Willie Mays, who did it all with flair, but Hank Aaron makes a strong case, too. Hammerin' Hank smacked 755 home runs, batted .305 over 23 seasons, won 3 Gold Gloves, and led the league's outfielders 3 times in double plays.

Mickey Mantle and Roberto Clemente, contemporaries of Mays and Aaron—were also five-tool players. Mantle wasn't called the "Commerce Comet" for nothing. Clemente's glittering career was cut short when a plane crash ended his life just three months after he stroked his final hit—No. 3,000—in 1972. He was only thirty-eight years old. Roberto topped the .300 mark 13 times, won 4 batting crowns, and led outfielders in assists 5 times.

The best "five tool" player playing today is Ken Griffey Jr. He roams center field like a New York cop, possesses a laser-like arm, is speedy enough to take the extra base, and hits for power and average. He has averaged 35 home runs and a .300 batting average during his career, and he won 10 consecutive Gold Gloves in the 1990s.

After Griffey, it doesn't take the teacher very long to call roll. What do you think? Are the following players legitimate five-tool players? The hot stove league is open.

> **SAMMY SOSA.** If Sammy can hit for power and average like he did in 1998 (66 home runs, .308 average) for a couple more seasons, he could supplant Michael Jordan as Chicago's greatest sports hero. Nobody patrols the friendly confines of Wrigley Field better than Sammy, but he's a lifetime .267 hitter.

> **MARK McGWIRE.** He's the greatest home run hitter of our time, but Mark's no gazelle on the base paths, and he's not

likely to tag up on a shallow fly ball hit to right. The St. Louis Cardinal first baseman is surprisingly nimble in the field, however.

⮞ **BARRY BONDS.** Before knee and wrist injuries took their toll, Bonds was the best five-tool player in the game. He is one of four players to hit 300 home runs and steal 300 bases. He's earned 8 Gold Gloves playing in the swirling winds of 3Com Park (formerly Candlestick Park). Interesting trivia: his godfather is Willie Mays.

Willie Mays can do the five things you look for in a player—run, catch, throw, hit for distance, hit for average—better than anybody I ever saw.

NEW YORK GIANTS MANAGER
LEO "THE LIP" DUROCHER

Other current players who may have the five tools are:

• Vladimir Guerrero, the talented Montreal Expo outfielder who enjoyed a "breakout" season in 2000.

• Derek Jeter, the smooth-fielding Yankee shortstop who's learned to hit for average.

• Ivan Rodriguez, the Texas Rangers catcher who sprays doubles to the alleys and guns down runners with regularity.

• Alex Rodriguez, the tall, rangy shortstop who bats cleanup for the Texas Rangers and can play a step deeper because of his strong arm.

These five-tool players are known for their versatility on the diamond, but what about us? What makes a "five tool" Christian?

This is someone who:

1. Makes God's Word a priority.

2. Knows he can't grow without the fellowship of other believers.

3. Prays regularly.

4. Talks about his relationship with Christ to others, when appropriate.

5. Stays humble and loves others the way Christ loved us.

Baseball players must make the best of whatever natural tools they have been given. Only a select few are born every generation with the ability to be five-tool players. Christians, on the other hand, can be five-tool followers of Christ every time they step inside the lines. Why should we ever choose to be average?

Sammy Sosa

Since you have purified your souls in obeying the truth through the Spirit in sincere love of the brethren, love one another fervently with a pure heart.... Therefore, laying aside all malice, all deceit, hypocrisy, envy, and all evil speaking, as newborn babes, desire the pure milk of the word, that you may grow thereby.

1 PETER 1:22; 2:1–2

3rd Inning

Top of the Third
WHAT SHAPE ARE YOU IN?

 **I'**ll never forget one of my first baseball heroes as I grew up in the 1960s—Mickey Mantle, the larger-than-life New York Yankee who played centerfield with grace and majesty.

Mickey, a golden-haired country boy from Oklahoma, was blessed with lumberjack forearms and lightning speed. During his rookie season in 1951, manager Casey Stengel pronounced Mickey "the star of the future," a switch-hitting Triple Crown threat who would rewrite the record books.

Mickey made good on those predictions. His finest season came in 1956 when he won the American League Triple Crown with 52 home runs, 130 RBIs, and a glittering .353 batting average. Because he hit the ball so far, the phrase "tape-measure home run" was introduced into the national lexicon. Newspapers around the country printed grainy photos of Mickey launching a pitch high into the second deck of Griffith Stadium, home of the Washington Senators. The photos showed the arc of the ball reaching the nether regions, 565 feet from home plate. Another explosion, this time at Yankee Stadium in 1963, struck the park's right field façade. If the ball had kept sailing, it would have landed 602 feet from home plate.

For all of his home run prowess, few baseball fans remember that Mickey constantly battled injuries over his career. During his rookie season, Mickey tripped over an exposed drainpipe in Game 2 of the World Series, tearing cartilage in his knee, which caused him to miss the rest of the Fall Classic. In the 1957 World Series, Milwaukee second baseman Red Schoendist came down on Mickey's right shoulder while turning a double play. Both injuries dogged him for the rest of his career.

Unfortunately, Mickey's body also endured abuse from another source. He became fast friends with Whitey Ford and Billy Martin,

Yankee teammates who fortified their diets with generous amounts of adult beverages. Mickey became a switch-hitting drinker who could pour it down with either hand. Whitey once quipped, "Everybody who roomed with Mickey said he took five years off his career." Mickey and Billy Martin kidded each other about whose liver would go first.

One reason for Mickey's drinking was his suspicion that he would follow his father, grandfather, and two uncles to an early grave. His father, Mutt, died of Hodgkin's disease at the age of forty, and his grandfather and two uncles also succumbed to the same disease before they turned forty.

The way to make coaches think you're in shape in the spring is to get a tan.

WHITEY FORD

This former MVP was also MIA on the home front. He married Merlyn in 1952 and fathered four sons, but his long absences, coupled with his desire to spend more time with his drinking buddies than his family, caused huge rifts. His drinking problems worsened after he left the game in 1969. Life became a nonstop series of celebrity golf tournaments and memorabilia shows where he autographed anything thrust in front of him for $25 a pop. Alone on the road, with little to do during his free time, Mickey found solace in the bottle.

Meanwhile, he continued living, much to his chagrin. At age forty-six, he joked, "If I knew I was going to live this long, I would have taken better care of myself."

Mickey's story raises an interesting point. Are you taking care of your body? Did you know that 2 Corinthians 6:16 says, "For you are the temple of the living God"? That means taking care of your "temple" by eating in moderation and exercising regularly so that God can use you for many, many years of productive ministry.

And how are you caring for your spiritual body? Are you making it a priority to deepen your relationship with God? Are you caring for your soul by getting to know God better and trusting Him at all times? Are you staying in shape through regular Bible reading and church attendance?

Mickey's story has a happy ending. This Yankee great accepted Christ on his deathbed just before cancer claimed his life in 1995. The fact remains, however, that he wasted many years in the spiritual minor leagues when he could have been playing alongside Jesus Christ all along.

Are you going through life figuring that you can get in better spiritual shape sometime in the future? God is ready right now!

Or do you not know that your body is the temple of the Holy Spirit who is in you, whom you have from God, and you are not your own? For you were bought at a price; therefore glorify God in your body and in your spirit, which are God's.
1 CORINTHIANS 6:19–20

Bottom of the Third
RABBIT EARS

n Candlestick Park's early years, a charter bus driver who drove groups to every San Francisco Giant game liked to sit in the field level seats just to the right of home plate.

This man was armed with a bullhorn voice that could have guided ships past the Golden Gate Bridge. Instead of yelling encouragement for the home team, however, he gave Willie Mays "the business" every time No. 24 came to the plate.

"Heeeeeey, Pop-Up Mays!" he'd yell. "Heeeeey, Pop-Up Mays!"

Willie dug a hole in the back of the batter's box and pretended not to notice what everyone within earshot of home plate could hear. Even the scribes in Candlestick's press box could hear Mr. Foghorn.

"Heeeeeey, Pop-Up Mays!"

After one exasperating afternoon, a beat writer asked Willie, "Buck, can you hear this 'Pop-Up Mays' character when you come to bat?"

"Yup, I can hear him," said Willie, who told friends that he could hear Mr. Foghorn in his sleep.

Throughout the history of baseball, the great players have been the ones who learned to block out trash-talking opponents and the taunts of irritating "fans" in the grandstands. When Jackie Robinson broke the color barrier in 1947, he smoldered while enduring racial insults from fans and fellow players alike. Hank Aaron received "hate mail" by the sackful while chasing the most cherished record in sports: Babe Ruth's 714 home runs.

Today's ballplayers are not immune from razzing. Just ask some of baseball's good guys—Mark McGwire, Randy Johnson, and Tony Gwynn—who have encountered their share of catcalls over the years.

Fellow players also berated these future Hall of Famers. These "bench jockeys"—opposing players who rode them for everything they were worth—needled, ridiculed, and even questioned their ancestry. Why? Because bench jockeys want them to take their minds off the game and lose their concentration, taking their eye off the ball.

The world is trying to take your eye off the goal as well. These bench jockeys and bleacher bums—managed by Satan—are jeering you with taunts, such as:

- "No one will notice."
- "You only live once. Go for the gusto."
- "Your wife isn't what she used to be."
- "It's just a drug. No one gets hurt."
- "Too bad the kids are tying you down."
- "You can handle another drink."

> *Don't worry, the fans don't start booing until July.*
>
> EARL WEAVER

We must not be distracted by the gibes and Bronx cheers from Satan and the world he controls. That is more easily said than done, of course, but if we recognize Satan's trash talk for what it is and ask God to close our ears to his untruths, we can go about our business of leading a godly life.

Put away the "rabbit ears" and listen only to the One with pure speech: Jesus Christ.

Be sober, be vigilant; because your adversary the devil walks about like a roaring lion, seeking whom he may devour. Resist him, steadfast in the faith, knowing that the same sufferings are experienced by your brotherhood in the world. But may the God of all grace, who called us to His eternal glory by Christ Jesus, after you have suffered a while, perfect, establish, strengthen, and settle you.

1 PETER 5:8–10

4th Inning

Top of the Fourth
LEADING OFF
FIRST BASE

hen Maury Wills scratched and clawed his way to the big leagues in 1959 after toiling in the minors for eight and a half seasons, the stolen base had become a forgotten art. The last base stealer of note, Ty Cobb, set the major league mark of ninety-six steals in 1915, but the Georgia Peach was more famous for sliding cleat-high and slashing infielders with spikes filed to razor sharpness. With the elimination of racial barriers in the 1940s and 1950s, however, brilliantly talented black and Hispanic players added an exciting new dimension of speed and power to the game.

One of those speedy young players was Maury Wills, a slender Dodger shortstop who resurrected the "straight" steal at the Los Angeles Coliseum. Some nights, more than ninety thousand fans filled the cavernous Coliseum because major league baseball was new to the West Coast; the Dodgers had moved from Brooklyn in 1958.

The newly minted Dodger fans loved watching Maury inch off first base, standing in a crouch with his arms dangling at his side, while the pitcher looked nervously over his shoulder. As Maury stretched his lead, nearly 100,000 voices rose in crescendo, yelling "Go! Go! Go!"

The hapless pitcher, feeling like a pawn, delayed the inevitable by pivoting and throwing over to first. Maury always got back easily until he took larger leads—and ratcheted up the pressure. A quick throw over, a head-first slide, and a bang-bang tag play— "You're safe!" yelled the umpire—caused Dodger fans to go "OOOOOOOOH!" This meant that Maury had reached his maximum lead.

With the crowd noise creating a din, Maury crept off first base again. At the right moment, he was gone. He swiped fifty bases in

1960, his first full season, shattering Jackie Robinson's 1949 team-record of thirty-seven. When Maury stole his fiftieth base at the Coliseum, Dodger officials stopped the game and pulled second base from its moorings and handed it to the theft king.

Fifty stolen bases turned out to be a good start. Two years later, Maury attacked one of baseball's longest-standing records—Ty Cobb's ninety-six steals—and stole 104 bases, shattering the old mark.

> *There is always some kid who may be seeing me for the first or last time. I owe him my best.*
>
> JOE DIMAGGIO

Maury did it by studying pitchers' moves and by taking a lead from the back edge of first base. The way Maury figured it, first base was fifteen inches wide. If he took his lead from the back edge and the first baseman was standing at the front edge, that gave him an extra fifteen inches to get back, or an extra half step. An extra half step was often the difference between a stolen base and getting gunned down.

Maury's success resulted from his diligence in studying pitchers and in looking for a one- or two-foot advantage before a base-stealing attempt. In a similar vein, we need to pay attention to Satan's "moves"—moves he used against Adam and Eve in Genesis 3 and tried to employ against Jesus in Matthew 4. We should observe how Satan tempted Eve by questioning God's character, casting doubt on His goodness. We should observe how he appealed to her desire to be like God, the center of all things. We should look for those same kind of temptations in our lives and recognize them for what they are—the enemy's moves. We should stand on God's truth and rely upon the righteousness given to us in Jesus Christ.

Make no doubt about it: Satan has a sneaky move to first, but if we lead off with God's truth, trusting in faith that He won't let us get too far from the bag, we will get the green light to run for God.

Ken Griffey Jr.

Finally, my brethren, be strong in the Lord and in the power of His might. Put on the whole armor of God, that you may be able to stand against the wiles of the devil. For we do not wrestle against flesh and blood, but against principalities, against powers, against the rulers of the darkness of this age, against spiritual hosts of wickedness in the heavenly places.

EPHESIANS 6:10–12

Bottom of the Fourth
DÉJÀ VU ALL OVER AGAIN

 f there was ever a catcher I wish I could have thrown to, it would have been Lawrence "Yogi" Berra, the Yankee Hall of Fame catcher who squatted behind the plate from 1947 to 1963 and managed the New York Yankees and New York Mets to league championship pennants.

What a character! His cherubic face, adorned with craggy features and bushy black eyebrows, was "beautifully ugly," as one scribe wrote.

Although he spoke a "dese" and "dose" English learned from his Italian immigrant parents, he was known as a thoughtful, intelligent ball player, despite the limitations of an eighth-grade education.

What made Yogi special was his ability to say something funny or farcical without batting an eye. Maybe it was his lack of formal education or the charming way he spoke without thinking about the import of his words.

Yogi became known as the master of the malaprop, the father of the faux pas. Something would leave his lips, and everyone would laugh, causing Yogi to wonder why. A typical Yogism: "You can observe a lot just by watching."

Other examples include:

- "When you come to a fork in the road, take it."
- "Yogi, what time is it?"

  "You mean right now?"
- When talking about a popular restaurant named Charlie's, Yogi said, "No one goes there anymore—it's too crowded."
- At Yogi Berra Day at Yankee Stadium, Yogi said to fifty thousand fans, "I want to thank everyone who made this day necessary."
- When Yogi arrived fifteen minutes after a scheduled 4 p.m. appointment, he said, "Gee, Joey, that's the earliest I've ever been late."

On a hot day in St. Petersburg, Florida, Yogi Berra was dressed to the nines—beige slacks, matching polo shirt, and white loafers—while he stood outside Al Lang Field, minding his business.

Two older women walked by and recognized the famous face.

"Good afternoon, Mr. Berra," said one grandmotherly type. "My, you look mighty cool today."

"Thank you, ma'am," Yogi grinned. "You don't look so hot yourself."

Back in the 1960s, Yogi's wife, Carmen, called Yankee Stadium to tell Yogi that she was taking the Berra children to see *Dr. Zhivago*.

"What's wrong with dem kids now?" Yogi asked.

Yogi's most classic statement—"It ain't over till it's over"—will follow him to his grave and probably end up on his tombstone. Yogi may not be aware of this, but there's a spiritual truth in those six words. I take great encouragement in "It ain't over till it's over" because it's a reminder that we're in this battle for the long haul.

Our lives are not a sprint—we are in a continual marathon. Living without my left arm for the rest of my days on earth sure looks like a marathon to me. (I have more than thirty years left if I live a normal

> *The trouble with baseball is that it is not played the year round.*
>
> GAYLORD PERRY

life span.) My left arm and part of my shoulder are gone, abruptly amputated before dangerous cancerous cells could infect the rest of my body. Since that appendage brought me so much joy and allowed me to play a boy's game in front of millions, I felt a deep emotional loss as well.

I had two choices after my amputation: I could either isolate myself from the rest of the world and wallow in self-pity, or I could bow my neck—as we used to say when a pitcher was in a tight jam—and go right after life. I have chosen to stay intense and remind myself that life isn't over until it's over. I know it's easy to say that, but I am on a journey that, quite frankly, I don't want to give up on. There will be a day when the Lord says it's over, but I want to battle until that day.

Each of us will face times when we feel like quitting. The daunting trials that you face may be physical like mine, or they may be emotional or spiritual. Whatever they are, remember that God will be with you and has promised to give you the strength to endure.

Therefore do not cast away your confidence, which has great reward. For you have need of endurance, so that after you have done the will of God, you may receive the promise.

HEBREWS 10:35–36

5th Inning

IT'S STILL CHEATING,
EVEN IF YOU DON'T GET CAUGHT

 **P**layers call it "getting an edge," but that's just glossing over what it really is: cheating. From filling hollowed-out bats with cork to scuffing baseballs with emery boards to replacing base paths with beach sand, both players and management have long sought to tilt the odds in their favor. So what if those practices are unethical? Baseball operates under an unwritten rule penned by sportswriter Heywood Broun in 1923: "Do anything you can get away with."

Pitchers, the fraternity I belonged to, have bent the rules or broken them with impunity throughout baseball's history, all in a mad desire to pitch a ball that does everything but sit, beg, and roll over. By the time baseball reached the Roaring Twenties, "trick" pitches had gotten out of hand. Pitchers routinely doctored the ball with spit, mud, tobacco juice, or whatever else was on hand, or they scuffed up the ball's leather covering with their belt buckles.

After a "loaded" Carl Mays pitch struck Ray Chapman in the solar plexus in 1920—and killed him—the major league baseball rules committee outlawed all tampering with the ball. Their edict hasn't stopped many pitchers from seeking an unfair advantage, however. Consider these attempts:

- Gaylord Perry shined up the ball with so much Vaseline that he had the audacity to entitle his autobiography, *Me and the Spitter.*

- Umpires busted Joe Neikro when a five-inch emery board and small piece of sandpaper mysteriously fluttered to the ground.

- Rick Honeycutt sliced baseballs with a thumbtack sticking through a Band-Aid on his finger.

- Jim Bunning, a U.S. Senator from Kentucky, used a grinding machine in a back room at Tiger Stadium to file his belt buckle to razor sharpness.

Branch Rickey claimed that he could teach anyone to throw the spitball in fifteen minutes. A pitcher starts by licking his forefinger and middle finger with a generous helping of saliva—not enough liquid to drip off his fingers but more than enough to turn a page of this book. Next, he grips the ball like he's going to throw a fastball, but he makes sure his first two fingers are not placed across the seams. As he goes into his windup and releases the ball, the pitcher attempts to "squirt" the ball from his fingers, much like pinching a slippery watermelon seed at your brother.

A guy who cheats in a friendly game of cards is a cheater. A pro who throws a spitball to support his family is a competitor.

GEORGE BAMBERGER

The ball will travel toward home plate with little or no spin like a knuckleball, but just as it reaches home plate, the ball will drop like it fell off a table. Even if batters are expecting a spitball, they will swing and miss or top the ball into a harmless infield grounder. Since it's usually obvious that a pitcher has just thrown the devilish spitter, he usually refrains from going to the saliva buds until he *really* needs an out.

I've seen spitballs thrown in pressure-packed situations. I've seen teammates strike out because they swung at an unhittable pitch. I strongly feel, however, that no pitcher ever gets away with cheating.

Deep inside, they know their careers are tainted. They know that they could have never accomplished what they did on the mound unless they willingly broke the rules.

You've probably never had the opportunity to scuff a baseball, but maybe you nicked the taxman by claiming deductions not allowed by the IRS. Whether you're cutting corners or cutting baseballs, cheating leaves us with the same sense of guilt.

Some cheaters may never be exposed in this life, but all will be exposed on the Day of Judgment. Second Corinthians 5:10 says we must all appear before the judgment seat of Christ to answer for our lives. That should be a chilling thought—especially for those thinking about "getting an edge."

Alex Rodriguez

Do not be deceived, God is not mocked; for whatever a man sows, that he will also reap. For he who sows to his flesh will of the flesh reap corruption, but he who sows to the Spirit will of the Spirit reap everlasting life.

GALATIANS 6:7–8

Bottom of the Fifth
HITTING IS SUCH A HARD THING TO DO

I'm certainly happy that I didn't have to hit to earn a living. My lifetime batting average of a buck twenty-five (.125) is actually pretty good for pitchers, so I'm not ashamed of my batting skills. If my career had depended upon my hitting ability, however, I would have been looking for another line of work very quickly.

Ted Williams said that hitting major league pitching is the single most difficult assignment in professional sports. Batters are asked to swing a

36-ounce bat with a round hitting surface that cannot be more than 2.75 inches in diameter onto a moving ball with a diameter of 3.38 inches. Compared to other ball-strike sports such as golf and tennis, baseball is unusual in that its hitting instrument is smaller than its target.

Who am I to argue with Ted Williams, considered by many to be the best pure hitter of all time? Teddy Ballgame compiled a glittering .344 lifetime batting average, which means he failed nearly two-thirds of the times he strode to the plate. In what other sport can you fail 67 percent of the time and be rewarded with a $100 million contract?

Nobody confused me with Randy Johnson when I was in my prime, but the Jugs speed gun clocked me in the high eighties and low nineties. Even my turtle fastball reached the plate in .41 of a second, which didn't give the batter much time to react. An 80 mph changeup or slow-breaking curve ball also arrives at the plate in a hurry—.50 of a second or half a second. Batters have around .13 of a second to decide whether to swing from their heels or check their swings if they judge the ball to be outside the strike zone.

That's why baseball is not a game of inches, as Branch Rickey once said, but a game of milliseconds and millimeters. Batters must employ incredible hand-eye coordination to strike such a fast-moving object at just the right instant. The difference between hitting a line drive single or missing the ball entirely is almost immeasurably small, but you also have to be incredibly strong to jack the ball beyond the outfield wall. If you want to match Mark McGwire in the home run department, plan on meting out 1,400 pounds of force to hit the ball 400 feet.

Okay, so I never hit a ball 400 feet, but I did jack a ball out of the park. My only major league home run came in San Diego against Dennis Powell of the Los Angeles Dodgers. I sent his 3-2 offering over the 375 sign in the left-centerfield alley and rounded the bases with a huge grin. An ironic footnote is that we lost the game 2-1, meaning I provided the only offense for the Padres that day.

Maybe I should have thrown a shutout in that game. Anyway, I loved to take my hacks. Although I averaged only one hit for every eight times at bat, I never paid much attention to my batting average because I was a pitcher. Everyday players, however, understand how important stats are when it comes to hitting, and I saw dozens of players fret after every 0-for-4 evening.

When I get the record, all it will make me is the player with the most hits. I'm also the player with the most at bats and the most outs. I never said I was a greater player than Ty Cobb.

PETE ROSE

These players, for the most part, are trying to measure up to a standard, and that standard says if you are a .300 hitter, you are one of the best. I've seen many Christians try to measure up to God's standard, which is 1.000, or perfection. Sorry, but it can't be done.

Batting one thousand in the game of life is just not possible, but that still doesn't keep many of us from trying to follow every do and don't of the Christian life. Through my experiences, I've discovered that God just wants me to love Him more and more each day, not focus on how "good" I've been. I will never measure up perfectly to Him.

Byron Ballard led me to the Lord back in 1981 when we were both playing in the minor leagues. I'll never forget what he once said to me: "When you get to the major leagues, Dave, remember that Jesus is your only audience."

You know what? What Byron said helped me recognize that I was put on this earth to please God and nobody else. He doesn't care if I bat a buck twenty-five or pitch five no-hitters or even a perfect game—He just wants me to love Him and worship Him as the Creator of the universe.

That sounds like a base hit to me.

Jesus said to him, "You shall love the Lord your God with all your heart, with all your soul, and with all your mind. This is the first and great commandment."

MATTHEW 22:37–38

6th Inning

Top of the Sixth
HOME SWEET HOME

id you notice that few ballplayers shed any tears when the San Francisco Giants moved to Pacific Bell Park and McCovey's Cove, watching windblown Candlestick Park as it was left behind in their rearview mirrors?

I can't say I don't blame them. Built on a landfill abutting San Francisco Bay, Candlestick's weather conditions created either a cold, fog-enshrouded venue or a blustery ballpark better suited for flying kites than playing major league baseball games. The 'Stick was home to a microclimate in which cool winds swept over the western foothills and swirled through the park before whipping up whitecaps in San Francisco Bay.

In Candlestick's early days, the Giants players wore turtlenecks and kept hot water bottles on the bench—even in July. The temperature two miles inland could be eighty degrees, but at the water's edge, howling, biting gales kept Candlestick in a freezer box. The prevailing winds knocked down long fly balls at the warning track, which probably cost Willie Mays a serious attempt at Babe Ruth's home run record. I never heard the Say Hey Kid complain, however.

Candlestick's notorious history passed through my mind when I learned that I had been traded to the Giants in 1987. I'll never forget manager Roger Craig sitting down the players and saying, "Gentlemen, regardless of how you have felt about Candlestick Park in the past, this is our home, and we will like it." Roger recognized the psychological edge that a home team could enjoy in our ballpark, which is why he attempted to instill the right attitude about Candlestick Park into the players.

Inspired by Roger's pep talk, I decided I would use the adverse weather to work in my favor. That meant pitching the right-handed hitters inside and pitching left-handed hitters outside because the prevailing winds blew in from left field. If the wind happened to turn around and blow in my face, I knew I could get more action on my sinking fastball because of the added wind resistance.

Once I carried a good attitude to the mound, I *loved* getting the call to pitch in Candlestick. I loved it when I heard hitters moan, "I hate hitting in this park." That's like starting each at-bat with a 0-1 count. By using Candlestick's breezy conditions to my advantage, I compiled a 10-4 win-loss in that park. Put another way, one-sixth of my lifetime wins came in a park with a reputation for blowing distracting hot dog wrappers through the air and pitchers off the mound. (Remember Stu Miller in the 1962 All-Star Game?) I pitched well because I believed that Candlestick Park would determine whether I succeeded or not, and that's an attitude I've carried over to the rest of my life.

> *When Neil Armstrong set foot on the moon, he found a baseball that Jimmy Foxx hit off me in 1937.*
>
> LEFTY GOMEZ

You see, it doesn't matter where God has you at this moment. You may think that your present job is the pits, or where you live is a terrible part of town, but God has you where He wants you to be—for the moment. He can do great things with you right where you are. Pastor and author Chuck Swindoll says life is 10 percent of what happens and 90 percent

Tony Gwynn

how you react to those situations. How are you reacting to the situations God has placed you in? Are you grumbling like visiting players, or do you have the same sunny disposition that Willie Mays had?

Also keep in mind that God won't keep you where you are forever. My three seasons with the Giants went by like a twenty-four-hour white sale, and your circumstances could change tomorrow. Until then, be content as you await for what God has in store for you.

. . . be content with such things as you have. For He Himself has said, "I will never leave you nor forsake you."

HEBREWS 13:5

Bottom of the Sixth
LIKE FATHER, LIKE SON

ave you noticed how many of today's players have fathers who also played in the big leagues? What makes me feel old is that I played against most of their fathers!

Take Ken Griffey Jr., the only son ever to play with his father, Ken Griffey Sr., in a major league game. The Griffeys were inserted into the Seattle Mariner lineup on August 31, 1990, thus becoming the first father-and-son teammate combination in major league history. What a mind-boggling accomplishment!

Close to thirty major leaguers these days have fathers who played in the bigs—an amazing statistic. With thirty teams carrying twenty-five players each, that creates a pool of 750 major league players. This means 4 percent of the planet's best baseball players had fathers who played major league baseball. I find this to be astronomically high when you consider that the odds of someone putting on a major league uniform and actually getting into a game situation has been estimated to be .00004 percent, or 1 in 25,000. Yet one in every twenty-five players has a father who played. (I know. I'm starting to sound like a *Bill James Baseball Abstract*.)

Let's take a look at some of the more well-known father-son combinations.

- Ken Griffey Jr. and his father, Ken Griffey
- Roberto and Sandy Alomar Jr. and their father, Sandy Alomar
- Barry Bonds and his father, Bobby Bonds
- Moises Alou and his father, Felipe Alou (Moises was once managed by his dad at Montreal.)
- Eduardo Perez and his father, Tony Perez
- Todd Stottlemyre and his father, Mel Stottlemyre (presently a Yankee pitching coach)

- Todd Hundley and his father, Randy Hundley
- Bret and Aaron Boone and their father, Bob Boone

The Boones are actually the first three-generation family to play in the big leagues. Ray Boone, an American League catcher in the late 1940s and '50s who fathered Bob Boone, is the grandfather of Bret and Aaron Boone.

To what can we attribute so many father-son combinations? Answer: a gene pool populated by .300 hitters and winning pitchers. These sons are in the game because their bodies were blessed with a piece of their father's talent. Think about it: these fathers couldn't spend much spare time with their kids while they were playing major league baseball nearly eight months a year. Besides, more than half of their time was spent on the road when you include spring training. Sure, these kids got to hang around a major league clubhouse and soak in the atmosphere of the Show, but they are where they are today through inherited talent and a willingness to work hard. It certainly helped to have a famous father to imitate.

People ask me what I do in winter when there's no baseball. I'll tell you what I do. I stare out the window and wait for spring.

ROGERS HORNSBY

We, too, have a Father worth imitating. Our ultimate desire should be to become imitators of Him. As I've tried to imitate Christ, I've had to ask myself these questions:

- Am I loving others the way Jesus would like?
- Am I forgiving people the way Jesus would forgive them?
- Am I passionate about life in the way Jesus was passionate about life?
- Do I have the strength to face the toughest stuff in life in the same way that Jesus did?

If we're going to get down to brass tacks, that's what living is all about—being imitators of the One who gave us the greatest example. As you seek to follow the example of Jesus Christ, remember the tremendous resources available to you.

Romans 8:9 reminds us that if we belong to Jesus, then His Spirit will live in us. In addition, don't forget that it is God's plan to conform us to the image of His Son. In baseball terms, this is like having an Almighty Father who guarantees that we will make it to the major leagues. With confidence, we can follow in the footsteps of our Lord.

And be kind to one another, tenderhearted, forgiving one another, just as God in Christ forgave you. Therefore be imitators of God as dear children. And walk in love, as Christ also has loved us and given Himself for us, an offering and a sacrifice to God for a sweet-smelling aroma.

EPHESIANS 4:32–5:2

7th Inning

Top of the Seventh
THE RELIEVERS

n some ways, I'm glad I wasn't a major league pitcher one hundred years ago. If I had been, I think my left arm would have *fallen* off before it was amputated.

During baseball's "dead ball" era, starting pitchers such as Cy Young and Christy "Matty" Mathewson were expected to play the entire game— all nine innings, win or lose. Matty and New York Giants teammate Joe "Iron Man" McGinnity pitched 800 innings in 1903, or 63 percent of the club's total, to lead the National League in innings pitched. As a way of contrast, the most innings I ever pitched was 215 with the San Diego Padres during the 1985 season.

The way old-time managers saw it, if the game went into extra innings, you simply kept on hurling; you certainly didn't complain that your arm was getting sore. To do so was to admit weakness, and managers equated a pitcher's stamina with moral quality. Those who couldn't "cut the mustard" until the final out were disparaged as "seven-inning pitchers"—players who didn't have what it took to straddle the rubber with the game on the line.

John McGraw, the New York Giants skipper who managed the club from 1901 to 1932, was one of the first to recognize the folly of having his front-line pitchers continue to throw until their arms drooped. Midway through his managing career, he started inserting relief pitchers into the game sooner than his contemporaries. *Better to win ball games with a fresh arm standing on the mound in the late innings,* he thought, *than having a tired starter hanging on, trying to prove that he still had "his stuff."*

The last McGraw starter to lead the league in innings pitched was Christy Mathewson in 1908. By the 1920s, his pitchers were nowhere near the league leaders in innings pitched. McGraw had several live arms waiting in the bullpen, itching to get into the game. With an experienced relief corps, fewer pitchers went for complete games.

When McGraw started managing at the turn of the century, 90 percent of ball games ended with complete games. By the 1930s, that figure dropped to 50 percent as managers began to see the wisdom of sending in their ace reliever to get the final outs. Today's game has evolved to the point where managers routinely employ "set-up" relievers in the seventh and eighth innings to "set the table" for the feared "closer." No wonder the complete game statistic has fallen to less than 5 percent.

> *A boy cannot begin playing too early. I might almost say that while he is still creeping on all fours he should have a bouncing rubber ball.*
>
> CHRISTY MATHEWSON

As for me, I finished my career with just twenty-eight complete games out of approximately 218 games started. Did that make me less of a pitcher? Of course not. The fact is that when I passed the 110 to 120 pitch count, my effectiveness waned. My role as a starting pitcher was to keep the game close if we were behind and extinguish any rallies if we were leading. I knew there were guys in the bullpen—like Goose Gossage in San Diego—who were capable of coming in and closing the door.

When I was in the battle for my life against cancer, I had people come in from the bullpen when I needed a break. My wife, Jan, was the long reliever who didn't bail out on me, even though I wouldn't have blamed her if she had. My parents and brothers were my middle relievers whose constant support reminded me that life was worth living, even in the midst of much pain and suffering. And I'll never forget my "short relief pitcher," a great friend named Sealy Yates who flew from the West Coast to spend three days in my New York City hospital room, maintaining a twenty-four-hour vigil. Sealy could have remained home in California in his comfortable bed, but he chose to sleep on a cot in my room and stay by my side during a difficult surgery.

I didn't have to go for a complete game all by myself. I found that when God says, "I will never leave you nor forsake you," He uses people to keep that promise. You are certainly a person God wants to use to bring comfort and encouragement to others. You can be a relief pitcher, coming in to help a brother who appears to be running out of gas and needs a hand.

Do you know a family member or close friend who is stressed, burdened, or struggling to get through life? If so, you might be just the right reliever.

And let us consider one another in order to stir up love and good works, not forsaking the assembling of ourselves together, as is the manner of some, but exhorting one another, and so much the more as you see the Day approaching.

HEBREWS 10:24–25

PLAYING ON THE
GOD SQUAD

early ten years before I joined the San Francisco Giants, much was written about the "God Squad" of Christian ballplayers playing on the team. The bulk of the newspaper reporting was not positive press, however. Sports scribes sharpened their quills and dissected the outspoken Christian athletes, taking great pains to point out the hypocrisy of Christian ballplayers who preached one thing but did another.

With that as a backdrop, I remember the time when I was given an opportunity to talk about my faith with a teammate. Most ballplayers don't want to hear you mention Jesus Christ's name unless it's used in a profane way, but on this occasion, I had my teammate's ear. He genuinely wanted to hear what it meant to be a Christian.

After being an attentive listener, he said, "I have no problem with believing what you say about God and Jesus Christ."

"Good," I said. I took the opening to explain my faith in greater detail. Then I asked, "Would you like to ask Christ into your life and know that you will spend eternity with Him?"

"No, this is where it stops for me," he said.

"Really?"

"Yeah, really. I have a problem with Christians."

"Why's that?" I gently probed.

"Part of the reason I choose not to become what you guys claim to be—born-again Christians—is because you are nothing but a bunch of hypocrites."

I nodded, inviting him to continue.

"They're out carousing. They drink a lot. They use four-letter words. They cheat on their wives."

I winced. My teammate was correct, I had to admit. "You're right; they do all those things," I said, shaking my head in disgust.

"The only thing I can say is that these baseball players are not the object of our faith—Jesus Christ is."

"Yeah, well they can stuff it," said the ballplayer, who stood and left.

I grieved that afternoon because my teammate was right. Hypocrisy is a cancer that weakens our ability to share our faith with others. Sure, high-profile figures such as an unscrupulous televangelist, or an untruthful ministry leader, or a pious-yet-philandering ballplayer can hurt the cause of Christ, but every individual Christian is being watched by friends and neighbors as well. People around us notice how often we skip church, sprinkle our speech with four-letter words, share the latest off-color joke, or verbally cuff our spouses and kids in front of others.

Sports do not build character. They reveal it.

JOHN WOODEN

We are all under the magnifying glass, which means we must be careful that we walk the talk. I was certainly tested in my playing days. I remember sitting in front of my locker one day, minding my own business while I quietly dressed for the game. Suddenly, a teammate tapped me on the shoulder and asked me to turn around. With a leering grin a mile wide across his face, he held a *Playboy* magazine in his hands. It was opened to the centerfold model, and he stuck the glossy picture in my face.

Then there were guys who literally tried to drag me back to the training room after the game for a few beers. "It's not going to hurt," they said. I declined those drinking sessions, not because having one beer is a sin, but because I didn't want to compromise my Christian witness to them.

At the same time, I made sure that I did not alienate myself from my teammates. Whenever another player asked, "Hey, Dave, want to join us for something to eat?" I usually joined them. I knew drinking would occur, but I wanted to show them that I could have a good time without chugging fresh drafts. My body language said, "Even though I may not drink like you drink, I still respect you for who you are."

That's one of the vital life lessons I want to impart in this book. Many of our non-Christian friends think we're hypocrites, and that's an unfortunate thing. The challenge for us is to live a solid life that is pleasing to Christ, a life that will inspire others to ask us about our faith.

Bret Boone

Try instead to live in such a way that you will never make your brother stumble.

ROMANS 4:13, TLB

8th Inning

Top of the Eighth

THEY CALL HIM "THE IRON CHIPMUNK"

You just can't help but like Chad Curtis, the spunky utility player with the Texas Rangers. He wears a "What Would Jesus Do?" wristband during games and writes a column on the religion page of the *Arlington Morning News*. Talk about wearing your faith on your sleeve. Chad is a stand-up guy who doesn't take guff from anybody.

Perhaps that's because he battled his way to the major leagues, overcoming even longer-than-usual odds. Chad played college ball at Grand Canyon University, a small Christian college in Phoenix that played an NAIA schedule.

Chad was a big fish in the small NAIA pond, winning All-American and Scholar-Athlete laurels, but that didn't count much with the pro scouts. The Anaheim Angels drafted him in the forty-fifth round—an afterthought, to be honest—but within three years, he rose through the minors to become an everyday player with the Halos. After three years with Anaheim, he then bounced around the league with three other teams before landing in New York, where he became the Yankees' fourth outfielder.

Built like a fireplug and burning with intensity, Chad and his flattop haircut didn't back down to anybody—even his teammates. He had run-ins with Kevin Mitchell, a former MVP, and Derek Jeter, the celebrated Yankee shortstop. He criticized Jeter after a bench-clearing brawl between the Yanks and the Seattle Mariners, noting that Jeter was joking and "shadowboxing" with good friend Alex Rodriguez of the Mariners while his teammates were duking it out in the infield.

Chad entered our living rooms during the 1999 World Series when manager Joe Torre inserted him into the Game 3 lineup against the Atlanta Braves. Chad made the most of his chance, smashing two home runs, including his "walk-off" shot in the bottom of the tenth inning to win the game in dramatic fashion. After circling the bases to the cheers of the jubilant Yankee home crowd and being carried off the field by his teammates, Chad was ushered over for a quick "how-do-you-feel?" interview with NBC's Jim Gray.

Two days earlier, Gray had grilled Pete Rose on national television about his past association with gambling—a typical "ambush" interview we see so often on live telecasts. There was talk that the Yankee and Brave players were going to boycott any Jim Gray interview.

> *The Lord taught me to love everybody, but the last ones I learned to love were the sportswriters.*
>
> ALVIN DARK

At the crowning moment of his career—his fifteen minutes of fame after winning a World Series game with a home run—Chad informed Jim Gray and a national audience that he wasn't going to talk to him because of what he did to Pete Rose. "But I do want to wish my grandmother well in her surgery tomorrow," said Chad. With that, he waved to the camera and jogged into the locker room.

Six weeks after his heroics, Chad was traded to the Texas Rangers to ease the Yankee logjam in left field and cut salary costs.

It didn't take long for Chad to make his mark in Arlington. During the first month of the 2000 season, Chad got into a clubhouse scuffle with teammate Royce Clayton. The reason? Chad was bothered by the lyrics and the volume of a rap song blaring from Clayton's boom box—a nasty number called "The Thong Song"—mostly because children were walking around the locker room prior to the game.

"We live in a society that wants to practice tolerance and acceptance, which at the root is a good idea," Chad told reporters. "But you step back sometimes and say, 'What is it that we tolerate? What is it that we are accepting? Is anything acceptable?' My answer to that is, no, not everything will be tolerated.

"I'm just a person who decided that if there's something worth standing for, I'll stand for it. If there's a guy in the stands cussing with little kids nearby, I'll go tell him he's being a poor role model."

Way to go, Chad. Those are wise words from a ballplayer—words I couldn't have said better myself.

The Lord is good, a stronghold in the day of trouble; and He knows those who trust in Him.

NAHUM 1:7
(ONE OF CHAD CURTIS' FAVORITE VERSES)

Bottom of the Eighth
SANDY KOUFAX, MY HERO

eople often ask me who my baseball idol was when I was growing up. That's an easy one to answer: the great Sandy Koufax of the Los Angeles Dodgers.

One of the things I loved about him—besides the fact that he was left-handed—was the way he delivered the ball to home plate. Sandy straddled the rubber, then went into his windup, bringing his hands over his head before coiling into a high leg kick. His pitching motion was clean and smooth. Sandy was not a big man, but his small, wiry frame could generate ninety-five mph gas.

Growing up, I just loved No. 32 from the Los Angeles Dodgers. My dream was to become a major league pitcher, and Sandy Koufax was the player I emulated. I was crushed, however, when he suddenly retired at the age of thirty following the 1966 season. His 27-9 record couldn't be touched, but traumatic arthritis in his left elbow drove him from the game he loved. He moved to a country homestead in Ellsworth, Maine—about as far as you can move from glitzy Southern California. Sandy did a half-dozen seasons of commentary work for NBC's "Game of the Week," but he never felt comfortable sharing about himself when asked. He quit the broadcast business with four years left on his contract.

The only time he appeared in public was during spring training when he visited with Dodger pitchers as a roving instructor. I saw him hanging around the batting cage a few times, but I could never summon the courage to approach him and introduce myself.

Then in 1994, I was invited to speak at the Final Four in Charlotte, North Carolina, where the University of Arkansas and the Duke Blue Devils were paired off in the Monday night final game. In the Charlotte Coliseum that night, I saw celebrities and dignitaries everywhere. Even President Bill Clinton was in attendance since his Razorbacks were playing for the NCAA national championship.

When I spotted Sandy Koufax across the arena, I was just floored. I nudged my wife, Jan, and said, "Hon, you're not going to believe this, but Sandy Koufax is over there."

"Well, why don't you go over there and say hello to him?" said Jan matter-of-factly.

"There's no way I could go over there. I mean, this guy was an icon to me."

"Look, just do it," said Jan. "He's not going to bite you."

I walked across the arena to his section, which was crawling with security.

A guard stopped me. "Look," I explained, "I'd like to go over and say hello to Sandy Koufax."

> *I became a good pitcher when I stopped trying to make them miss the ball and started trying to make them hit it.*
>
> SANDY KOUFAX

"I'm sorry," replied the guard, "but this is a secured area. The President's up in that skybox, so I can't let you in."

Now, you have to know I never, ever do this, but I looked at him and earnestly said, "Sir, my name is Dave Dravecky. I used to pitch for the San Francisco Giants. I was diagnosed with cancer. I came back after ten months of rehabilitation to pitch in the big leagues again; then five days after that I fell and broke my arm. Sandy Koufax was my hero growing up, and all I want to do is go over and shake his hand."

The guard looked me over, amputation and all. "Bud, with a story like that, go right ahead," he said.

I walked over to Sandy Koufax and stuck out my right hand. "Sandy, my name is Dave Dravecky, and I just wanted to come over and say hello because when I was growing up, you were my hero."

A genuine look of surprise came over Sandy, who appeared to be in his late fifties. "Dave, how are you doing?" he asked. "I have followed your story for a long time, and I hope everything's okay."

We had a wonderful chat, and afterward I could have floated out of the arena. Spending a few moments with Sandy Koufax was an incredible moment in my life, which is why I believe every kid needs a hero, someone to look up to.

Isn't it interesting that my visit with Sandy was so memorable that years later I can still remember the euphoria of that evening? Yet I have the opportunity to spend time every day with my eternal hero, Jesus Christ, and so do you.

Don't get me wrong: there's certainly nothing wrong with having human, earthly heroes like Sandy Koufax. We can learn much from great role models like this former Dodger great, but fixing our attention on Jesus is even better. Spending time with Him can renew our minds and prepare us for the challenges of daily living. While it was a thrill meeting my boyhood baseball hero, I find happiness in knowing that I have an even greater hero in my life: Jesus Christ.

One thing I have desired of the Lord, that will I seek: that I may dwell in the house of the Lord all the days of my life, to behold the beauty of the Lord, and to inquire in His temple.

PSALM 27:4

9th Inning

Top of the Ninth
DON'T FORGET
TO TOUCH THEM ALL

 he 1999 National League Championship Series was contested between two teams that hated each other's guts— the Atlanta Braves and New York Mets. The reason I remember this classic series so well is not what Braves reliever John Rocker said about the rabid Mets fans but how Game 5 ended.

Let me set the stage. The New York club had dumped the first three games to the rival Braves, but after winning Game 4, the Mets believed they had a shot to become the first team in major league history to come back from a 3-0 deficit.

Game 5 was played at boisterous Shea Stadium. It was a nip-and-tuck affair that stretched into extra innings. In the bottom of the fifteenth, with the score 4-4 and the bases loaded, Robin Ventura blasted a Kevin McClinchy pitch over the center field wall to dramatically win Game 5 by the score of 8-4.

But wait a minute. Ventura never reached second base because his jubilant teammates tackled him and carried their home-run hero off the field. I was stunned. Why didn't the Met players wait until Ventura touched home plate before mobbing him?

Scorer Red Foley, in conjunction with National League officials, had no choice but to rule that Ventura's home run was a single, thus making the final score 5-4. Ventura didn't think anything of it. "As long as I touched first base, we won," he said. "Maybe tonight, when you guys [the media] go home, I might run the bases."

Sorry, but the game was over. Fortunately, Robin's action didn't affect the final outcome of the game, but a different base-running miscue way back in 1908 did. Nearly one hundred years later, it is still remembered as the "Fred Merkle bonehead" play.

Late in the '08 season with just a dozen games left, the New York Giants were battling the Chicago Cubs for the National League pennant. Before a boisterous crowd at the Polo Grounds, the Giants and the Cubs struggled to a 1-1 tie through eight-and-a-half innings. In the bottom of the ninth, the Giants started to rally. With two out and Moose McCormick on first, Fred Merkle singled to right, allowing McCormick to take third base. Now there were men on first and third, two out.

> *Close don't count in baseball. Close only counts in horseshoes and grenades.*
>
> FRANK ROBINSON

The next batter, Al Bridwell, singled up the middle into center field. McCormick trotted into home with the winning run to the sheer delight of the Giants fans.

Fred Merkle started for second base, but the minute he saw the ball roll up the alley, he turned and lit out for the Giant clubhouse, which was beyond the right center-field fence. In those early days of baseball, the ushers at the Polo Grounds opened the gates from the stands to let the fans pour out and greet their heroes on the field. The players, who didn't like getting mobbed, were used to running like the dickens for the safety of the clubhouse once the game was over, which was

Merkle's goal. But Cubs second baseman Johnny Evers saw that Merkle hadn't touched second base. He retrieved the ball (most baseball historians believe the original ball was tossed into the stands, so he found another ball), touched second base, and searched for the umpires' dressing room to plead his case. He and Chicago manager Frank Chance claimed that Merkle was out on a force play, negating the Giants run, meaning the game was still 1-1.

Umpire Hank O'Day ruled that indeed Merkle was out, but since the field was still the scene of joyous mayhem, he suspended the game. League officials deliberated three *days* before deciding that the tie game would have to replayed as a playoff game after the season, if necessary.

Wouldn't you know it? The Giants and Cubs ended the season tied for first, the Cubs won the replayed game, the Giants lost the 1908 pennant, and baseball writers wrapped the "bonehead" moniker around Fred's neck for the rest of his life.

The moral of the story? Always run out the play. Follow the rules. The temptation to take the short cut, the easy way out, is often strong. For Fred Merkle, it seemed much easier to just head for the clubhouse and buck the masses of fans on the field rather than run out the play. Few shortcuts have been as notorious as his, but many have been just as disastrous.

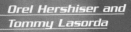

How many church leaders in recent years have taken the "easy way out," but ended up destroying their ministries and their families? Remember the story of King Saul in the Old Testament? He started well but became impatient and decided to do things his way rather than God's. In the New Testament, the apostle Paul referred to a colleague named Demas who ministered at his side, but when the going got tough, Demas took the easy way out and abandoned Paul.

You may be presented with the opportunity to take the "easy way" regarding sexual pleasure or making a few extra dollars. You know it's not God's way, but who will ever know, right? Fred Merkle never thought anyone would notice his shortcut either, but someone did.

Today and every day, run out every play. Finish the race that God has put before you.

I have fought the good fight, I have finished the race, I have kept the faith. Finally, there is laid up for me the crown of righteousness, which the Lord, the righteous Judge, will give to me on that Day, and not to me only but also to all who have loved His appearing.

2 TIMOTHY 4:7–8

Bottom of the Ninth

THE SHOT
HEARD 'ROUND THE WORLD

Why do baseball pundits become absolutely teary-eyed when recalling the 1951 season? Reason: the New York Giants executed the greatest comeback in baseball history to catch the arch-rival Brooklyn Dodgers at the pass, and then the "Jints" bested "da Bums" in a best-of-three playoff series capped by the "Shot Heard 'Round the World."

It is worth savoring every morsel of the Giants comeback. New York began the season as a so-so club until Willie Mays was called up on May 25. The twenty-year-old rookie center fielder, however, reacted to big league pitching like a deer caught in the headlights of a Mack truck. Willie went 0-for-12 in his first dozen major-league at-bats and practically begged Giants skipper Leo Durocher to send him back to the minor leagues. Then he drove a Warren Spahn pitch into the upper deck for his first major-league hit, but he slumped again, slipping to a basement batting average of .039.

After one disastrous outing, Durocher found Willie sitting in front of his locker, bawling his eyes out. "I'm sorry, Mr. Leo. Send me back down. I told you I couldn't hit big league pitching. Send me back down, Mr. Leo."

Remember, baseball's color line had only been broken four years earlier. Leo was a cocky, loudmouth white manager, and Willie was a precocious young black player—scared and intimidated by the bright lights. Leo put his arm around his young charge's shoulder. "Look, Willie. You are my center fielder. Today. Tomorrow. For as long as I'm managing this club. Now stop your crying," he said softly.

Willie and his teammates were still thirteen-and-a-half games out on August 11 when they pieced together their amazing comeback. While the Dodgers played .500 ball, the Giants went on a 37-7 tear and caught Brooklyn on the final day of the season. In those pre-divisional days, a tie prompted a three-game playoff series. The Giants and Dodgers split the first two before playing the decider at the Giants' home park—the Polo Grounds, a quaint, bandbox stadium with "low shelf" left-field grandstands that stood just 315 feet from home plate.

The National League pennant race of 1951 belongs to the ages. There has been nothing like it before or since. Nor will it come again. Summarizing the 1951 race is akin to summarizing King Lear. Before anything else, your effort will diminish majesty.

ROGER KAHN

The Dodgers erupted in the eighth inning with three runs to break a 1-1 tie. In the bottom of the ninth, Brooklyn led 4-1 and was just three outs away from a "Subway Series" date with the New York Yankees. The Giants needed four runs to win, three runs to tie. In baseball, this is what's known as *There's no tomorrow. Do or die.*

Alvin Dark's infield single led off the Giant ninth. He took third on Don Mueller's single, raising hopes among the Giant faithful. Clean-up hitter Monte Irvin dampened those when he popped up in foul territory.

But Whitey Lockman's clutch double scored Dark and sent Mueller to third. Now the Giants were down 4-2, and a single would tie the game.

Dodger manager Charlie Dressen dipped into the bullpen and handed Ralph Branca the ball. While he warmed up, the Giants next batter, Bobby Thompson, was called over by manager Leo Durocher.

"If you ever hit one," he said, "hit it now."

Bobby nodded and didn't say anything. He knew he was excited, but he was probably not half as excited as the nervous Willie Mays standing in the on-deck circle.

Branca took his warm-up pitches, and then Thompson stepped in. Branca kicked and delivered a high fast ball for a called strike. Ahead in the count, he thought about throwing the next pitch slightly out of the strike zone, anticipating that an eager Thompson would swing at it. Then he would come at him with a curve low and away.

On the second pitch, Branca made the delivery—a fast ball up and over the middle of the plate. Thompson swung hard and met the ball cleanly. The low line drive rocketed into the left field grandstands, and like a thunderclap, the Giants had beaten the Dodgers.

Giants announcer Russ Hodges screamed, "The Giants win the pennant! The Giants win the pennant! The Giants win the pennant!" as if that had been the most foreign thought just ten seconds earlier. The home

crowd roared in delirious delight as Thompson circled the bases. In the blink of an eye, everything had changed for the Giants.

In the blink of an eye, everything will change when we enter God's presence for eternity. What a priceless treasure! While we're still here on earth, life sometimes feels like we are down three runs in the ninth inning, like we have no hope, no future. But we do, thanks to something far greater than the "Shot Heard 'Round the World"—the resurrection of Jesus Christ. Jesus' resurrection completed the greatest come-from-behind victory in the history of creation. Jesus was victorious over death, and we will be, too, when we pass from this life to the next. Let that "Good News" be heard around the world!

And I heard a loud voice from heaven saying, "Behold, the tabernacle of God is with men, and He will dwell with them, and they shall be His people. God Himself will be with them and be their God. And God will wipe away every tear from their eyes; there shall be no more death, nor sorrow, nor crying. There shall be no more pain, for the former things have passed away." Then He who sat on the throne said, "Behold, I make all things new."

REVELATION 21:3–5

Extra Innings

LITTLE LEAGUE
BASEBALL

 think youth baseball—Little League, Pony League, Mustang League—is wonderful. One of the great joys of my post-baseball years was coaching my son's Little League team in Colorado Springs. So what if some of our springtime ballgames were called off because of snow? There was something special about seeing my third-grade son, Jonathan, stroking a Texas Leaguer over the second baseman's head.

One of the best Little League stories I've heard comes from Bob Welch, an excellent author from Eugene, Oregon, who has written several books, including *A Father for All Seasons*. One summer, his son Jason was a seventh-grader playing in a seventh/eighth grade league. At that age, some kids have gone through puberty and sport five o'clock shadows, while others could try out for the Vienna Boys Choir and still hit the high notes.

Jason Welch was one of those apple-cheeked kids still waiting for his growth spurt. At four-feet, nine-inches, he stood a good foot shorter than many of his contemporaries, but this kid had game. As we said in the big leagues, Jason was going to the plate to take his hacks.

One Saturday afternoon, little Jason found himself standing in the batter's box against the tallest, meanest pitcher in the league, a right-handed fireballer who stood twelve inches taller than Jason.

The eighth-grader went into his windup, kicked and fired a blazing fastball right down the pike. Jason never moved an inch. "Strike one!" the umpire bellowed.

The second pitch scorched across the plate. Again Jason didn't budge. "Strike two!" yelled the ump.

The chatter from both sides reached a crescendo. The lanky pitcher reared back and threw his third pitch. The ball came right at Jason. He turned to avoid being hit, and then fell to the ground like he had been shot. His bat went flying. His helmet bounced around in the dirt. The ball seemed to have skimmed his shoulder.

"Take your base," the umpire announced.

Jason's father, standing in the third base coach's box, took several steps toward plate just to see if Jason was alive. When he stood up and dusted himself off, Bob expected his son to take his free base.

But wait a minute.

"It didn't hit me," Jason said to the ump.

"Take your base, son," said the ump.

"Really, it didn't hit me."

> *I think it's wonderful—*
> *it keeps the kids*
> *out of the house.*
>
> YOGI BERRA,
> ON THE MERITS OF LITTLE LEAGUE BASEBALL

Bob, meanwhile, was thinking what any baseball parent would think in such a situation: *Take your base, son. You've been wounded, soldier; your war's over. You're going home.*

"Honest, it didn't hit me," Jason pleaded.

The umpire, hands on his hips, looked at Jason and then to the infield ump, who just shrugged. "Okay," said the ump, "the count is one-and-two."

Bob wondered if he should call time out and intervene. But Jason was already digging his rubber cleats in the batter's box.

The towering pitcher rocked and fired. He hurled a bullet down the middle—the kind of pitch that would send most kids to the dugout.

Instead, Jason stepped in and ripped the ball into left-center field for a stand-up double. His teammates and parents roared, including the father standing in the third-base coaching box.

Just a few steps away from Bob stood the manager of the team in the field. He had no idea that the four-foot, nine-inch seventh grader standing on second base was Bob Welch's son. The manager spit out his sunflower seeds and slowly shook his head.

"Man," he said, "you gotta love that."

Yup, you gotta love it when unexpected things happen. The great news for believers in Jesus is that as we walk with God, little miracles happen all the time. Every day we face battles similar to those that Jason faced, and sometimes we get knocked down, but Jesus is always there to help us to our feet, dust us off, and encourage us to get the hit that everybody thinks is impossible.

You gotta love that.

Then David said to the Philistine, "You come to me with a sword, with a spear, and with a javelin. But I come to you in the name of the Lord of hosts, the God of the armies of Israel, whom you have defied. . . . Then all this assembly shall know that the Lord does not save with sword and spear; for the battle is the Lord's, and He will give you into our hands."

1 SAMUEL 17:45, 47

IF IT WEREN'T
FOR BASEBALL . . .

f my life could be summed up in one at-bat in the big leagues, then I could say my life was like watching a towering home run sail into Busch Stadium's Big MacLand's third deck, section 383. In my career, I got to touch all the bases: eight years as a major-league pitcher. A World Series start. My "Comeback" game against the Cincinnati Reds. Winner of the 1989 Hutch Award, which honors the memory of former Reds manager Fred

Hutchinson, who died of cancer in 1964. A 3.13 lifetime earned run average and an above .500 win-loss record. I still get asked to sign my own baseball cards.

Beisbol, as Sammy Sosa would say, *has been bery, bery good to me.* If it weren't for baseball, I wouldn't have met Byron Ballard, a minor league teammate on the Amarillo Gold Sox, a Double A team in the Texas League. Byron invited me to a baseball chapel, where I heard the Gospel presented in such clear terms that even a thickheaded baseball player like myself could understand my need for a Savior.

If it weren't for baseball, I would have never become a public speaker. Following the 1984 season, when the Padres won their first National League pennant in franchise history before losing to the Detroit Tigers in the World Series, I was asked by the Padres to join their speaker's bureau.

"But I've never spoken before a group," I replied. Like 95 percent of Americans, the thought of public speaking terrified me.

"We need someone who can represent the Padres this winter before community groups, civic organizations—whatever," said the Padres team official. "We think you will do a wonderful job."

I began standing up and addressing every Rotary Club and high school sports banquet out there—the "rubber chicken circuit" we called it. Little did I know that God was preparing me for a speaking ministry.

If it weren't for baseball, I never would have met Myles Gentzkow, the chapel coordinator for the Padres, who challenged me to share my testimony with others. I'll never forget the first time I shared my faith at a Youth for Christ event at Point Loma Nazarene University in San Diego—or the humbleness I felt when others decided to trust in Jesus after hearing my story.

If it weren't for baseball, I would have never met Alex Valhos, a twelve-year-old boy diagnosed with leukemia. During my "Comeback" game, KNBR, the flagship radio station for the Giants, asked listeners to donate money for every pitch I threw and register for a national bone marrow match program. More than $115,000 was raised that day, and seven thousand people signed up for the bone marrow registry. I don't know how many lives were saved over the years, but, unfortunately, we couldn't save Alex. He died two years after my final "Comeback" pitch.

If it weren't for Alex, however, I don't know whether Jan and I would have ever started the Outreach of Hope ministry for those fighting cancer. We didn't know it at the time, but God used baseball to make divine appointments with our lives time after time, pitch after pitch.

Your role in life probably will not include a career in baseball. Whatever God calls you do, He has a way of orchestrating the good and the bad that happens in your life and making a symphony out of it. The final result: beautiful music.

Yes, *beisbol* was very, very good to me, and if you look at life from God's perspective—His big picture—life will be very, very good to you.

Jan and Dave Dravecky

. . . for it is God who works in you both to will and to do for His good pleasure.

PHILIPPIANS 2:13

Extra Innings
"OH, DOCTOR!"

f you're a major league radio announcer, you must demonstrate the verbal adroitness of a Pedro Martinez splitter and
the split-second decision-making of a plate umpire. Then
again, if you're Jerry Coleman, the San Diego Padres radio announcer
since 1972, you don't have to demonstrate any of these qualities. You can
speak without thinking. Say the first thing that comes to mind.
Experience a disconnect on live radio. When Jerry does any of those
things, we hear a "Classic Colemanism"—and share a chuckle.

Jerry, who was a fine second baseman with the New York Yankees in the 1950s, was the Voice of the Padres during my playing days in San Diego. He's still calling them the way he sees them, which is both frightening and delightful at the same time.

Everyone loves Jerry, who is well into his seventies and is still the Friars main play-by-play man. But I can't help but wonder if people are drawn to the radio like they are drawn to a train wreck. Just sit back and enjoy this sampler of Jerry's verbal miscues:

- "Winfield goes back to the wall. He hits his head on the wall and it rolls off! It's rolling all the way back to second base! This is a terrible thing for the Padres!"

- "It's a base hit on the error by Roberts."

- "From the way Denny's shaking his head, he's either got an injured shoulder or a gnat in his eye."

- "Johnny Grubb slides into second with a standup double."

- "All the Padres need is a fly ball in the air."

- "Davis fouls out to third in fair territory."

- "There's a shot up the alley. Oh, it's just foul."

- "That's the fourth extra base hit for the Padres—two doubles and a triple."

- "Houston has its largest crowd of the night here this evening."

- "Last night's homer was Willie Stargell's 399th career home run, leaving him one shy of 500."

- "The first pitch to Tucker Ashford is grounded into left field. No, wait a minute. It's ball one. Low and outside."

- "That's Hendrick's 19th home run. One more and he reaches double figures."

- "Well, it looks like the All-Star balloting is about over, especially in the National and American Leagues."

- "The Padres, after winning the first game of the doubleheader, are ahead here in the top of the fifth and hoping for a split."

- "Mike Caldwell, the Padres' right-handed southpaw, will pitch tonight."

- "Reggie Smith of the Dodgers and Gary Matthews of the homers hit Braves in that game."

- "Gaylord Perry and Willie McCovey should know each other like a book. They've been ex-teammates for years now."

- "On the mound is Randy Jones, the left-hander with the Karl Marx hairdo."

- At Royals Stadium: "The sky is so clear today you can see all the way to Missouri."

- "They throw Winfield out at second, but he's safe."

- "Oh, Doctor!"

Vladimir Guerrero

Quotes

I told my general manager Roland Hemond to go out and get me a big name pitcher. He said, "Dave Wehrmeister's got eleven letters. Is that a big enough name for you?"
    —EDDIE EICHORN, Chicago White Sox owner

Jose Canseco leads off the third inning with a grand slam.
    —JOHN GORDON, Minnesota Twins announcer

He fakes a bluff.
    —RON FAIRLY, San Francisco Giants announcer

Last night, I neglected to mention something that bears repeating.
    —RON FAIRLY

How do you say adios in Spanish?
    —CLAY CARROL, Cincinnati Reds reliever

That's why I don't talk. Because I talk too much.
    —JOQUIN ANDUJAR, Houston Astros

There's one word that describes baseball—"You never know."
    —JOQUIN ANDUJAR

On Father's Day, we again wish you all happy birthday.
    —RALPH KINER, New York Mets radio announcer

The Hall of Fame ceremonies are on the 31st and 32nd of July.
    —RALPH KINER

If Casey Stengel were alive today, he'd be spinning in his grave.
    —RALPH KINER

The reason the Mets have played so well at Shea this year is they have the best home record in baseball.
    —RALPH KINER

Rome wasn't born in a day.
    —JOHNNY LOGAN, Milwaukee Braves shortstop

I'll have pie a la mode with ice cream.
    —JOHNNY LOGAN

I will perish this trophy forever.
    —JOHNNY LOGAN

I know the name but I can't replace the face.
    —JOHNNY LOGAN

No thanks. I don't drink.
    —PITCHER JEFF STONE, after being asked if he wanted a shrimp cocktail

PHIL RIZZUTO: *"Hey Yogi, I think we're lost."*
YOGI BERRA: *"Yeah, but we're making great time!"*

You better cut the pizza in four pieces because I'm not hungry enough to eat six.
    —YOGI BERRA

He must have made that before he died.
    YOGI BERRA on seeing a Steve McQueen movie

You got to be very careful if you don't know where you're going because you might not get there.
    —YOGI BERRA

Dave Dravecky's
OUTREACH
OF Hope

$\mathcal{W}$hile pitching for the San Francisco Giants during his seventh year in Major League Baseball, Dave Dravecky was diagnosed with a cancerous tumor in his pitching arm. The following years were a whirlwind of surgery, radiation, and depression—all in the glaring light of the media. Dave's arm was eventually amputated to stop the spread of the cancer. Throughout the experience, Dave and Jan's faith in God provided the anchor they needed in the storm.

During this struggle, Dave and Jan received thousands of letters and requests from hurting people who were encouraged by the Dravecky's faith. In response this outpouring of emotion, Dave and Jan founded the Outreach of Hope in 1991. The ministry's mission is to offer comfort, encouragement, and hope through Jesus Christ to those who suffer from cancer or amputation. This mission is accomplished by offering prayer support, non-medical referral services, and resources to cancer patients, amputees, and their families. In addition, support materials are available for churches, healthcare professionals, and individuals who work with those battling cancer.

Dave and Jan are also the best-selling authors of eight inspirational books. Recently, they served as general editors with Joni Eareckson Tada on *The Encouragement Bible*, a specialty Bible for people dealing with adversity. Further, they are both national speakers who address topics ranging from motivational to inspirational.

FOR MORE INFORMATION, PLEASE CONTACT

Dave Dravecky's
OUTREACH
OF *Hope*
13840 Gleneagle Drive
Colorado Springs, CO 80921

PHONE: 719-481-3528
FAX: 719-481-4689
E-MAIL: info@OutreachOfHope.org
WEB SITE: www.OutreachOfHope.org